50 THINGS ABOUT BIRDS IN MICHIGAN

C000076486

Birding in the Great Lake State

Kim Kaiser

Cover designed by: Ivana Stamenkovic
Cover Image: pixabay

CZYK Publishing Since 2011.
CZYKPublishing.com
50 Things to Know

Lock Haven, PA
All rights reserved.

ISBN: 9798429610122

50 THINGS TO KNOW
ABOUT BIRDS IN THE USA

If you know someone who loves birds, I cannot imagine them not learning or enjoying this book. This book is perfect for both experienced birders and beginners alike. It is written in readable prose and studded with personal stories from the author's many years of observing birds.

50 Things to Know About Birds in Pennsylvania: Birding in the Keystone State
Author Darryl & Jackie Speicher

I really enjoyed this book. I live in the Badger state and I learned a lot of things I didn't know before. The author got me excited about taking up bird watching. Definitely going to plan a day trip to Horicon Marsh.

50 Things to Know About Birds in Wisconsin : Birding in the Badger State
Author Carly Lincoln

Smart little book for my birding friend! Includes a clever guide for regional experiences!

50 Things to Know About Birds in Florida: Birding in the Sunshine State
Author Krystal Hickey

50 THINGS TO KNOW ABOUT BIRDS IN MICHIGAN

BOOK DESCRIPTION

If you have ever met someone from Michigan, they probably held up their palm and used it as a map of Michigan! The State of Michigan is comprised of two landmasses. The Lower Peninsula, which is roughly shaped like a mitten, and the Upper Peninsula, the land surrounded by Lakes Michigan, Huron, and Superior. With more coastline than any state except Alaska, Michigan is a major vacation destination for both in-state and out-of-state visitors.

There are so many opportunities to see exciting and unique birds in Michigan. Whether you are a passenger in a car, enjoying a morning coffee on your porch, or exploring the beaches and other remote areas of the Great Lakes State, you might see any of the more than 450 species of birds in Michigan. 50 Things to Know About Birds in Michigan hopes to whet your appetite to be on the lookout for birds as you live in or travel around our state.

Kim Kaiser has written 50 Things to Know About Birds in Michigan to supplement more traditional bird identification books. Even casual birders will use multiple books and sources to identify birds, and this book is not intended to replace any of those resources. But so often those books are focused entirely on what a bird looks like, and they give few details about the unique, secretive, or bizarre behaviors of those birds. Did you know that some birds use snakeskins to ward off predators? Or that some ducks you can see in Michigan nest in trees? 50 Things to Know About Birds in Michigan has gathered together an interesting fact about each bird described, something to help you remember or even seek out a place to observe some of these birds which you find particularly compelling.

Michigan is an important territory crossed by a substantial number of migrating birds who live in Canada and the Arctic. As a result, many birds can be seen in multiple regions of the state during their migrations north and south. This book is divided into 4 sections based on the most likely environments where you might see specific birds: Birds of the Lakes, Rivers, and Shores, Birds of the Open Fields, Farms, and Orchards, Birds of the Woodlands, and Birds of the Suburbs.

For species uniquely found in limited or protected locations, information is included to plan the best way to see those birds. Wilderness and other habitats set aside for birds and other wild animals are described. Otherwise, be ready to see many of these birds, incidentally, throughout Michigan.

On your way up north for fishing, hunting, or skiing, heading to sporting events in Detroit, visiting one of Michigan's premier universities, or just hanging out at home, 50 Things to Know About Birds in Michigan will help you recognize and appreciate the birdlife in the many natural habitats which epitomize the Great Lakes State.

TABLE OF CONTENTS

DEDICATION

This book is dedicated to my loving husband, David Fortin, who introduced me to the joys of birding and taught me how to properly use my binoculars.

ABOUT THE AUTHOR

Kim Kaiser has been writing about science, technology and the environment for 30 years. Most of her work has been done for private companies or institutions. 50 Things to Know About Birds in Michigan is her first published book.

Kim has lived in Michigan since 1979 and has been an enthusiastic follower of bird facts since 2000. She has had the opportunity to observe birds across the U.S., in Costa Rica, Botswana and Namibia. Her most exciting bird observation was the Long-tailed paradise whydah, seen at the Cheetah Conservation Fund near the Etosha National Park in Namibia. In 2020, she and David had a rare bird sighing (in our area) of a Vermillion Flycatcher.

Kim and David live in central Michigan where they enjoy watching Bald Eagles and Great Blue Herons fly past their living room window on the Chippewa River.

You can reach out to Kim at 50birdsmichigan@gmail.com.

INTRODUCTION

"When one tugs at a single thing in nature, he finds it attached to the rest of the world."

John Muir

Nowhere else in North America is the impact of glaciers more pronounced than around The Great Lakes State of Michigan. Glaciers carved out five enormous lakes and split the land into two masses: the Lower Peninsula and the Upper Peninsula (UP.) Blessed with more freshwater coastline than any other place in the world, Michigan is a premier destination for watersports, fishing, boating, and beachcombing. Prevailing weather creates a unique microclimate along the western, Lake Michigan side of the state, from Leelanau County to the Indiana border. Michigan is the world's largest cherry producer, and the orchards and farms in the flat lowlands around river bottoms make Michigan a leader in many other agricultural products.

A large fraction of Michigan's northern is still undeveloped, and after virtually all of the timber was logged in the 1800s, much of the woodlands have regrown. The southern Lower Peninsula is dominated by agriculture and urbanization. Michigan straddles the climate zone where deciduous trees give way to pine forests. The boundary between these regions transects the state diagonally from southeast to northwest. Leafy deciduous trees dominate the landscape of the south and central regions of the state, but as you travel north, deciduous trees give way to pines, spruce, hemlocks, and cedar. You find more birch trees, which thrive in areas where the ground remains frozen all winter.

Michigan is at the edge of two important migration routes in North America. It sits on the western edge of the Atlantic Flyway, and the eastern side of the Mississippi Flyway. Migrating birds are funneled into Michigan and along the Great Lakes coastlines. The consequences are some of the most spectacular birding sites on the continent. Each spring and fall, people gather from the 4 mile stretch of open water near the Detroit River to the Straits of Mackinac to see thousands and thousands of migrating raptors - hawks, eagles, osprey, and owls. Raptors fly the thermals down from Canada and need to find the shortest route across the water. Both of these areas make for spectacular viewing events during the spring and fall.

Near Detroit, check out the Lake Erie Metropark and Pointe Mouillee State Game Area. In the north, the Mackinac Straits Raptor Watch is a great resource for learning when species come through the area, and how to observe bird banding or participate in bird counts.

Southcentral and southeast Michigan is home to several locations where flocks of 1000s of Sandhill Cranes meet up and rest before the next leg of their migration. The Phyllis Haehnle Memorial Audubon Sanctuary near Waterloo Recreation Area in Jackson County is the largest roosting area for the cranes. Nearby Waterloo Recreation Area contains 3,000 acres of protected wetlands. The Baker Sanctuary and Kensington Metropark are prime areas for crane viewing.

In southwest Michigan, The Kellogg Bird Sanctuary is a prime area to see migratory waterfowl. Kellogg was also a key player in reintroducing Trumpeter Swans to the Midwest. Many species of ducks, herons, and other wading birds can be sighted.

In central Michigan, just south of Saginaw, the 10,000-acre Shiawassee National Wildlife Refuge is a designated Important Bird Area and sanctuary for the management of migratory birds. The number and range of birds using the sanctuary increase each year and a seasonally available self-driving tour is an excellent way to spend an afternoon.

The Allegan State Game Area in southwest Michigan contains the Kalamazoo River, which can be birded by canoe. Look for Prothonotary Warbler along the river, in addition to the Yellow-Billed Cuckoo, flycatchers, Red-eyed Vireo, and other wood warblers.

The Huron-Manistee National Forest in north-central Michigan is home to the iconic Kirtland's Warbler and the Hartwick Pines, one of only two places in the state where you can visit a stand of virgin forest and see what Michigan looked like before it was logged.

Further north is the Sleeping Bear Dunes National Lakeshore with 35 protected miles of Lake Michigan shoreline and both North Manitou and South Manitou Islands, which you can visit by ferry. There are 70,000 acres of dunes, forests, and rare beach vegetation. The Sleeping Bear Dunes are home to Michigan's largest breeding population of endangered Piping Plovers.

In the Upper Peninsula, the Seney National Wildlife Refuge has 5,000 acres of bogs, marshes, swamps, grasslands, and forest, and excellent bird watching opportunities from spring through fall. On the shore of Lake Superior in the eastern UP is Whitefish Point Bird Observatory.
Located in Michigan's eastern Upper Peninsula, the Whitefish Point area is famous for its impressive waterbird migrations.

Whether you seek out a special place to observe birds in Michigan, you are vacationing or traveling through the state, or you see birds in suburbs, parks or at backyard feeders, *50 Things to Know About Birds in Michigan* was written to increase your enjoyment of these delightful Michigan natural resources.

1. PIED-BILLED GREBE: WHAT ARE LOBED TOES?

There are five different grebe species in Michigan and the Pied-billed Grebe is common, albeit shy and not easy to find. Rarely seen in flocks, look for these small, brown, duck-like birds along the edges or in the vegetation on small marshy ponds, sluggish rivers, and lakes. When disturbed, it may sink slowly until only its head is above water or "crash-dive" and kick water in the air.

Grebes are often compared to Loons because both are excellent divers and have similar physical traits. The word grebe comes from a Latin word meaning "feet at the buttocks" and like Loons, it describes exactly where their feet are.

Grebes have lobed toes, which are toes with stiff scale-covered flaps that provide a surface similar to the webbing on duck feet.

Lobed toes create a larger surface area, but each toe is still separate. With their feet "at the buttocks", grebes are not good on land.

The Pied-billed Grebe eats large quantities of its own feathers and feeds them to newly hatched chicks. Biologists believe that the feathers form a sieve that prevents indigestible prey parts from getting into their intestines, and it helps form those items into pellets which they can regurgitate.

Male and female Pied-billed Grebes work together to build a floating mat-style nest and incubate their eggs. The young can swim soon after hatching, and often ride on both parents' backs when they are young, up to 3 weeks. They even hang on while adults swim underwater.

2. OSPREY THE MAGNIFICENT FISH HAWK

Ospreys return to the Great Lakes region early each spring and migrate away in the fall. This magnificent fish hawk is one of the birds you can see migrating as they cross over a 4 mile stretch of open water near the Detroit River. You can also see these distinctive raptors crossing Lake Michigan and Lake Huron at the Straits of Mackinac. The Straits are one of the best places in the country for seeing substantial numbers of birds of prey.

The return of Ospreys to Michigan is more than just the yearly migration. Ospreys were nearly wiped out in Michigan. Hunting and pesticides eliminated the species from the southern third of the state.

By 1998, there were a few clusters of Ospreys in the Upper Peninsula and northern Michigan. The Michigan Department of Natural Resources coordinated a reintroduction program, with help from many, many other organizations and dedicated volunteer citizen scientists. From 1998 to 2007, the Hacking Project had a goal of establishing 30 nesting pairs in southern Michigan. Hacking is a term covering the many steps used to raise and re-wild birds. Ospreys return to breed in the same place they hatched. Successfully raised on man-made towers, hacked chicks returned and established a natural pocket of Ospreys.

Ospreys are large hawks, smaller than bald eagles but larger than a goose. When you see it flying, the white underside and crook in its narrow wings help you to identify an Osprey. The head is white with a dark brown crown and a brown streak down the cheek. They are dark brown on the back and wings. Females are larger than the males; that's common for raptors.

Nest sites are at the top of large trees or other structures. Landowners and managed wildlife areas erect tall platforms for Osprey nests. They build a bulky pile of sticks, open to the sky. BIrds may use the same nest for years.

3. WOOD DUCKS ARE ORNATE GEMS OF NATURE

The first time you see a Wood Duck, I hope you can see it through binoculars. It is hard to imagine how ornately decorated male Wood Ducks are. Multiple colors and sharp lines make this duck look more like something created by an artist. A green head is decorated with a crest of darker feathers and a short orange bill, black on the tip. Beautiful blue and turquoise wings meet a green tail. The chest is chestnut brown and speckled with white dots, and the belly is a gentle buff-brown. Black stripes on the wings and neck look painted. And those red eyes – don't forget to check out the eyes!

Wood Duck hens are mottled brown and the perfect color for camouflage. Their eyes are black and ringed with white.

Wood Ducks are dabblers; they eat vegetation and love acorns, spending their summers nibbling at the edges of swamps, quiet

21

streams, beaver ponds, and woodland marshes. They're not likely to be found on a large stretch of open water. They are one of the few duck species with strongly clawed web feet, which they use to grip bark and perch on branches.

Wood Ducks nest in all 83 Michigan counties, in holes and natural cavities, in trees, or in nest boxes you see put up around lake edges. Wood Ducks choose a mate during the winter and arrive in the spring ready to mate and raise two broods. Plucky little Wood Ducklings jump from nests as high as 50 feet and make their way to the water, soon after hatching, with encouragement but no help from their mothers.

Wood Ducks migrate, and they begin arriving in Michigan in March. It used to be rare to see them, but with all the people putting up Wood Duck nesting boxes, they are becoming common even in more populated parts of the state.

4. THE COMMON LOON OF THE NORTH

In Michigan, the call of the Common Loon isn't as common as it used to be, but they still breed in the Upper Peninsula and very northern parts of lower Michigan. You can hear their haunting song at inland lakes which are large enough and deep enough for these iconic birds. Loon feet are located at the back of their bodies, and not underneath. Although their webbed feet are large, Common Loons rarely walk on land (except for nesting) and cannot take off from land. Loons run along the water, like an airplane, to gain speed for take-off.

Both males and females, in the summer, have black heads and necks with a necklace of black and white stripes. Their black and white checkered back and wings are breeding plumage. And in the summer, the eyes of the Common Loon are red. Experts think this is more for attracting mates than any visual specialty, although it may help them see better underwater. As the summer wanes eyes lose their red color and turn gray, and the black and white breeding plumage molts.

Common Loons are heavy, designed for efficient diving. They are very proficient fishers but need deep, clear water for success. While most birds have hollow bones, loons have solid bones and can compress their feathers and force the air out of their lungs, enabling them to dive for up to 5 minutes. Loons can submarine through the water with only their heads showing above the surface.

Loons migrate each fall to winter homes along the Atlantic Ocean or down the Mississippi Flyway to the Gulf of Mexico. In spring, as soon as the snow melts (and sometimes that means the very next day) loons return to their home lakes.

Loons are attached to their nesting lake and not to a specific loon partner. Nests are built near and often touch the water and are little more than bare ground when the eggs are laid. Both parents incubate the eggs and feed and defend their young.

Loons are a threatened species in Michigan, and the Michigan LoonWatch is a management, protection, and registry program of the Michigan Loon Preservation Association. Volunteer Loon Rangers are responsible for watching and protecting loons.

5. THREE SWANS IN MICHIGAN

Three species of swans are found in Michigan, the Trumpeter and Tundra are native species. The Mute Swan was introduced in the US in the 1800s and Michigan in 1919. Mute Swans were brought from Eurasia to decorate ponds and estates, but they escaped. Mute Swans are one of the most aggressive waterfowl species, especially while nesting and raising young. Mute Swans will chase native breeding birds from their nests. They are very destructive to native plants.

All three birds are white. The easiest way to tell them apart is by the color of their bills. Mute Swans have orange bills with a black knob on top. Trumpeter Swans have a solid black bill and Tundra Swans have a black bill with a small patch of yellow.

Tundra Swans stop in Michigan during their migration between Canada and the East Coast.

Trumpeter Swans by the thousands used to live on the Great Lakes. They were nearly wiped out in Michigan over 100 years ago. Their feathers were prized for hats or anything that needed their very soft and fluffy feathers. A decades-long effort by the W.K. Kellogg Bird Sanctuary at Michigan State University has helped bring Trumpeter Swans back to the Great Lakes. A captive breeding program was launched with eggs brought in from Alaska.

Trumpeter Swans have been observed nesting in the Shiawassee National Wildlife Refuge in central Michigan. Or look for them in ponds along the Au Sable River in northern Michigan.

6. PIPING PLOVERS SHARE OUR BEACHES

You probably will not see Piping Plovers in Michigan unless you seek out a special tour. That is the best plan if you are hoping for a rare chance to observe these critically endangered plovers in their wild Great Lakes habitat. The birds are slowly making a comeback in Michigan after nearly disappearing from their nesting and breeding grounds. They nest only in the Sleeping Bear Dunes and nearby dunes of Lake Michigan, and on the shores of Lake Superior. In the late 1980s, only a dozen pairs of these sand-colored small, stocky birds remained in the Michigan Great Lakes. The Piping Plover Recovery Plan is managed by the U.S. Fish and Wildlife Services with the objective of restoring and maintaining a viable population of piping plovers in the Great Lakes region.

Piping Plovers are small shorebirds and their pale color matches the white sand beaches. When in Michigan, they sport their breeding markings of a dark, narrow breast band and a dark stripe on their head. During the breeding season, they have bright orange legs. Plovers feed along the beach and mudflats, eating worms, crustaceans, and insects.

Piping Plovers lay their eggs directly on the sand, in a small depression, which they may reinforce with a few pebbles or shells. These nests are close to the water and very vulnerable to predators, rising water levels, and humans. They may abandon a nest if disturbed. Eggs are collected from abandoned nests, hand incubated, and then reintroduced by the Plover Project. Piping Plover chicks leave the nest soon after hatching and feed themselves, although they are closely tended by both parents. Habitat protection is the most critical goal of programs and people working to protect and restore Piping Plovers to Michigan.

7. PENGUINS IN MICHIGAN?

Am I serious? Yes, if you are near Detroit, you are near the largest penguin facility in the world! The Detroit Zoo in Royal Oak opened the habitats in 2016, and it's home to nearly 80 penguins. At the 33,000 square foot Polk Penguin Conservation Center you can see King Penguins, Rockhoppers, Macaronis, Gentoos, and Chinstrap Penguins up close.

When you first enter the facility, you are met with a 360-degree experience. Blasts of icy air and salty seawater mist set the arctic mood and remind you of the harsh environment where many of the world's penguins thrive. The interior is designed to recall the explorer Ernest Shackleton's ship, the Endurance, the three-masted ship Shackleton and his crew of 27 men sailed on their epic voyage to the Antarctic in 1914.

The Penguin Center is designed to resemble a glacier. Penguins dive and swim in their underwater gallery with huge acrylic windows and two acrylic tunnels. Visitors can see above, below, and around penguins in their 326,000-gallon, 25-foot-deep simulated sea. A section of glass flooring allows visitors to see penguins swimming below their feet.

In August 2020, King Penguins hatched a chick at the Detroit Zoo. The first time in 20 years!

8. PELICANS IN MICHIGAN: EXPECT TO SEE MORE

The American White Pelican winters along the southern U.S. coasts, and breeds across the north-central plains and Canadian. More and more, they are stopping to refuel in Michigan. In the early to middle of the last century, their numbers declined drastically, but they are rebounding. We'll start seeing them in a many more places during both the migratory and breeding periods.

Two reliable places to spot pelicans in Michigan are at the Pointe Mouillee State Game Area on Lake Erie, in Monroe County, and the Shiawassee National Wildlife Refuge, near Saginaw in central Michigan. It's exciting to see these very large waterbirds so far from the ocean. Shiawassee National Wildlife Refuge is open seasonally and has a driving path through the preserve.

Most pelicans are white with black flight feathers. They have large, webbed feet and a wingspan of 6 to 7 feet. They are unmistakable to identify, with a huge bill adapted with a gullet pouch to capture fish. The pouch is so sensitive that American White Pelicans can fish at night by "feel." To maintain their pouches, pelicans exercise the elasticity by throwing their heads back with the bill open or even by turning it inside out.

Biologists report that American White Pelicans have established a breeding colony in western Lake Erie for the first time, with possible future expansion into Lakes Huron and Ontario. It's exciting to see a bird species establishing new homes in Michigan.

9. HOODED MERGANSERS THE FISHING DUCK

Hooded Merganser are small diving ducks who use their strong feet and wings to dive underwater to catch fish. Mergansers are specialized "fish-eating" ducks. The edges of their long bills are serrated to help them grip slippery fish, and they have a third eyelid which helps them to see prey underwater. They also eat aquatic insects, crayfish, frogs, and vegetation. They are fun to watch diving underwater and guessing where they will pop up.

Both female and male Hooded Mergansers have a hood or crest of feathers, very prominent, that extends from the back of the head, like a hatchet. Males have a bold white hood rimmed in black and big white stripes on their backs; they really stand out. The female Mergansers' hoods are brown and look finer. Both have very long bills; the male's bill is all black, and the females are more muted, as is their general appearance. The hen is rich brown overall with a reddish-brown hood.

Some Hooded Mergansers stay here year-round, especially in the southern part of the state. In northern Michigan, you can find them from late March to mid-November. They arrive as soon as the ice has melted from lakes and ponds, with the mates they have selected the previous fall or winter.

Hooded Mergansers nest in tree cavities and use Wood Duck nest boxes, too. Like most ducks, mergansers often lay eggs in each other's nests, or different species may lay eggs in their nests. Within 24 hours of hatching the ducklings drop to the ground and may walk up to a mile to reach the water. They can dive and feed themselves instinctively; they chase and eat mostly insects when young. The females remain with their offspring for several weeks.

Look for mergansers in rivers, ponds, and streams throughout Michigan.

10. GREEN HERONS MAKE THEIR OWN LURES

Green herons are one of the small number of birds who make and use tools, and they use them for fishing. The small, solitary herons are bait-fishers and they create lures from insects, flowers, sticks, feathers, bread, and even plastic. They lay these items on the water's surface to lure small fish within striking distance. They join a small group of birds (crows, ravens, some types of parrots) who use tools to catch prey or obtain food.

I have seen Green Herons along quiet streams and shady riverbanks. The "green" color of their head and back is an iridescent color; they are mostly a dull blue-gray color, with a chestnut brown neck, and gray underneath. Look closer to see a white line down the front, short (for a heron) yellow legs, and a long dark bill with a sharp point. Fully grown green herons are about the size of crows. When hunting or baiting they hunch down and look much shorter.

The Green Heron is one of a group of similar small herons known collectively as green-backed herons. They may be found in any wetlands, lake, pond, marsh, or stream and are most active at dusk and dawn, so they can be difficult to spot. I often see Green Herons around bridges over small streams, where they probably are seeking shelter from the hot sun.

Unlike other herons, the Green Heron does not nest in large colonies. They nest in trees, usually near water, and avoid human disturbance. Both parents build the nest and incubate the 3 to 5 eggs. Once the young birds hatch, both parents continue to raise them.

In late August in Michigan, Green Herons head south, flying mostly at night to their winter homes in Mexico, Central, and northern South America. In April they head north again.

11. GREAT BLUE HERON

When I think about the Great Blue Heron, I am reminded of the rendering done by John James Audubon and how big that painting is. Audubon rendered his bird paintings at their actual size. Great Blue Herons are easy to spot hunting in ponds, marshes, inland rivers, and any quiet place along the water's edge. They specialize in hunting fish and other aquatic animals, but they are generalists and may eat other birds and small rodents.

I met one up close along the Lake Michigan shoreline, where a male Great Blue Heron had become habituated (used to humans) and it waited on the beach to grab the fish caught by people fishing from the beach. As soon as a fish was reeled in, the Great Blue ran in to grab it off the line.

All ardeids, the family which includes the herons, have a long slender neck with a characteristic S-shape. The anatomy of the neck is specialized; the bones create a coil in the neck which allows the birds to strike out at prey with incredible speed. The esophagus and trachea even run behind the vertebrae in the lower part of the neck, to protect them from damage and to provide the shortest possible route through the gullet.

Great Blue Herons are the largest heron in North America and a common resident of Michigan. They nest in trees, in colonies called rookeries. The females build the nest, a platform of sticks, normally quite high up in a tree, and it's very visible. One of the largest rookeries is in southeast Michigan, at Holland Ponds in Macomb County.

You can recognize a Great Blue Heron in flight and distinguish it from the Sandhill Crane by the position of the neck. Herons fly with a curved neck, while cranes fly with a straight neck. In the air, they are close in size and it's difficult to see the markings, but the neck position is quite obvious.

12. GREAT BLACK-BACKED GULL IS THE LARGEST GULL

The Great Black-backed Gull is more familiar on the northern Atlantic Coast but may be seen year-round in southeastern Michigan. In winter, these gulls are more widespread and may be spotted along any of the Great Lakes. Michigan is at the western edge of their range in the North. These are the largest gulls in the world.

They are aggressive birds who eat just about anything (fish, rodents, other birds) they can get in their mouth, and they steal food. They are pirates and scavengers and have benefited from human activity. They have learned to open hard-shelled mollusks and eggs by flying high and dropping them on rocks. Most foods are swallowed whole.

These are big birds with massive yellow bills. Adults have a white head, black upper parts, white underneath, and pink legs. They have wingspans of 4 to 5 feet.

Great Black-backed Gulls don't breed until they are 5 or 6 years old and they are long-living birds, some living twenty years or longer. They generally nest in colonies, mixed with other gulls and birds. Both sexes build the nest, on the ground, on, or near a rocky outcropping. They are devoted parents and both share brooding the nest and taking care of their young. They usually raise three chicks successfully each season; the young birds stay with their parents for up to 6 months.

Although they were hunted aggressively for their feathers, they have recovered and are especially tolerant and adapted to living near humans.

13. BELTED KINGFISHERS - FRIENDS OF THE RIVER

Belted Kingfishers are the only kingfisher species in Michigan and you can catch a glimpse of them along streams, rivers, and lakes.

Kingfishers are exciting birds who fly low and fast along the water and emit a loud and wild rattling call. They are related to the Laughing Kookaburra of Australia. They hunt by diving headfirst into the water from 20 to 30 feet heights, from perches, or by hovering over the water. Their long and narrow, sharp-pointed bill makes a deadly fishing spear. It's an apex predator of the watershed food chain.

Belted Kingfishers look a bit like Blue Jays; they have similar blue-gray colors but are about twice as large. They are stocky; their large heads are topped with a shaggy crest. They are powder blue above and white below with a blue breast band. In a case of reverse sexual dimorphism, females are more colorful than males with a rusty band across their belly.

Kingfishers nest in long tunnels excavated in the exposed vertical banks along watercourses. They create a chamber at the end of the tunnel and lay their eggs directly on the dirt. Both male and female Belted Kingfishers take turns incubating the eggs and feeding the hatchlings. Once they are old enough, kingfishers teach their young to hunt by dropping dead fish in the water for them to retrieve.

At the end of summer in Michigan, Belted Kingfishers migrate to winter homes in Mexico, Central America, northern Venezuela, and Colombia.

14. AMERICAN COOTS OR "MUD HENS"

Coots or "mud hens" are rugged, adaptable waterbirds we see in Michigan anyplace where we might see ducks. Coots are not ducks; they are related to rails, a secretive bird. But coots are happy to swim in the open or walk on land, so you might see them in city parks or on golf courses, as well as in rivers, ponds, and marshes. They travel in flocks and can be noisy and aggressive. When fighting for territory or mates, coots will rear up and attack each other with their big feet and lobed toes. Coots have lobed toes, instead of webbed feet common to other waterbirds.

American Coots come to Michigan to breed, and they require a fairly shallow freshwater area with access to lots of vegetation since they eat mostly plant material. Feeding methods include dabbling at the water's surface and upending to remain submerged longer and reach deeper. Hungry coots will also dive under the surface, graze on land, and even steal food from ducks.

They aggressively defend their nests, which they build in tall marsh vegetation in shallow water, a floating mat of dead cattails, and finer grasses. Coots may build more than one of these platforms and only use one or two for nests. Both parents build the platform and nests, and then take turns sitting on the eggs. Like ducks and other water birds, American Coot chicks are good swimmers soon after hatching and follow their parents in the water, returning at night to one of their floating platforms for cover.

15. COMMON TERNS: THE SEA SWALLOW

Common Terns are summer residents of Michigan's northern Great Lakes beaches. It's exciting to see these birds fish. They hover in the air over a school of fish; then with a sudden plunge, they seize fish with their bills. Sometimes they will dive entirely below the surface.

More decorative than other gulls and terns, they are white with a black cap, a pale gray back and wings, and red-orange legs and bill. In flight, their distinctive forked tail is displayed and you can see why this bird is called a sea swallow.

Like most larids (gulls and terns), they display a complex mating ritual. They begin in the air, with the females' zigzag gliding over the crouching males. Courting continues on the ground; males tip their heads down and hold their wings out from the body while walking around the female, who points her head upward. The male starts offering food, eventually feeding her exclusively.

Common Terns are gregarious, social birds living as flocks and breeding in colonies. They don't seem to enforce any particular pecking order. Each nesting bird is very territorial, even if that territory is just a couple of feet. The entire colony defends its territory against intruders, swooping and pecking humans and mammals which come too close. Before breeding begins, terns may "dread" or fly off the beach in unison to deter watching predators.

These shorebirds used to nest by the thousands along the Great Lakes' shores and islands. They need areas away from predators and humans because they nest directly on the sand. You can see Common Terns throughout the summer in northern Michigan and the Upper Peninsula.

16. ENJOYING MICHIGAN SANDPIPERS AND WADERS

Summer's end usually brings area lakes to their lowest levels. Submerged beaches and mudflats are now exposed and attract migrating shorebirds. A quiet paddle in a canoe or kayak at this time of year may reward us with groups of these probing shorebirds looking for mollusks, crustaceans, and insects.

Most shorebirds lack the bright colors and markings of familiar songbirds. Some of these shorebirds are seen only briefly in Michigan during spring and fall migrations. We don't have much time to get to know them before they are gone. An exception to that rule is the Greater and Lesser Yellowlegs. This trim and elegant wader draws attention to itself by bobbing its head and calling out loudly when approached. It's a brown and white speckled bird with light underparts and trademark yellow legs.

The Lesser Yellowlegs appear to be identical to the Greater Yellowlegs, just smaller. It's a more delicate bird; they don't winter as far north as the Greater Yellowlegs. Lesser Yellowlegs have lighter bellies and a shorter bill.

Our most familiar and successful shorebird is the Killdeer, which is a type of plover. It is successful because it has adapted to nesting near humans and even away from the shore. Sometimes Killdeer nest in gravel parking lots and on gravel roofs. It is famous for the broken wing act it performs to lure predators (and humans) away from its nest. The name comes from its loud call that seems to say "kill-deer, kill-deer, kill-deer."

The Spotted Sandpiper is the most common sandpiper in North America. Found along lakes and small streams, this is another brown speckled shorebird. One identifying marking is round spots on the breast which appear only in the summer. When it walks, it teeters as if it is just a bit too delicate. When startled it skims away low over the water.

The Spotted Sandpiper is a Michigan nester who turns the male/female script upside down with her polyandry. Females arrive first to the nesting area where they, and not the males, establish territory. She aggressively pursues the male and mates with three or four males a season, building one nest for each male she mates with and filling each with a clutch of eggs. The males incubate the eggs and care for the young.

BIRDS OF THE OPEN FIELDS, FARMS, AND ORCHARDS

17. BLUE ROBINS IN MICHIGAN? YOU ARE SEEING THE EASTERN BLUEBIRD

Eastern Bluebirds have always tolerated humans, and that is saving them. Those bird boxes you see placed on fences or other posts throughout the state are evidence of the bluebird conservation success story. Bluebirds are cavity nesters, but they don't have sharp bills like woodpeckers. They have always relied on cavities created by other birds or animals. Bluebird bills are specialized for catching insects or shucking seeds, not building.

When Europeans came to Michigan to log the forests, deep woods were transformed into open farm fields. People planted apple trees, which naturally have the crevices bluebirds need for nesting. Eastern Bluebirds thrived. Bluebirds' numbers declined in the last century

43

from the competition for a dwindling number of nest cavities from aggressive, non-native Starlings and House Sparrows. By 1930, their decline inspired Dr. Thomas Musselman to erect the first "Bluebird Trail" of over 1000 boxes near his home in Illinois. In 1970, Lawrence Zeleny wrote the landmark book *The Bluebird: How You Can Help Its Fight For Survival* and the North American Bluebird Society was formed.

The reason bluebirds are called blue robins is obvious. They have a chestnut throat and upper breast, and a white belly. They reminded early American settlers of English Robins. Males are uniformly deep, deep blue on top, females are grayer. Juveniles look like a completely different species (that's something they share with Robins) with a gray back, white eye-ring, and brown-spotted breast.

When breeding season is over, Eastern Bluebirds roam the countryside in small flocks before migrating south for the winter. They are Michigan residents from early spring until late fall. If you want to put up boxes for bluebirds, put them up in the fall or winter.

18. RING-NECKED PHEASANTS ARE A LONG WAY FROM HOME

Ring-necked Pheasants are an important game bird in Michigan, but did you know that they are not native to North America? These shy forest birds from Asia were first released in the 1700s in New York and New Hampshire. George Washington released pheasants at Mount Vernon. The Chinese Ring-necked Pheasant was introduced to Oregon in the late 1800s; by the 1930s this breed of pheasants was established from the Great Plains to the Atlantic coast.

Ring-necked Pheasants are shy birds who have adapted to the open country. Males are brightly colored with blue-green heads, red face wattles, and distinctive white neck rings. Females are plain buff-brown, and both have long, pointed tails. The legs and feet of this bird family are strong and well developed for walking. They prefer open grasslands, forest edges, and farmlands with mixed crops. Ring-necked Pheasants feed on the ground by scratching up insects, worms, and seeds. If they seem chicken-like, that's because they are in the same bird family as the common chicken.

Males take no part in incubation or raising chicks. Males crow to advertise their status and aggressively defend their territory and a harem of females.

Michigan's Ring-necked Pheasant population has sharply declined in recent years, due to the change in the way farmers raise crops. Instead of small farms and mixed crops, the practice of large, industrialized farms with a single crop means less brushy habitat for pheasants. Autumn plowing, which buries residual seeds and vegetation also negatively affects pheasants.

The Michigan Department of Natural Resources launched a program to encourage private landowners to create and improve environments for food, nesting cover, and winter cover, to restore and maintain Ring-necked Pheasants. With proper permits, pheasants can be raised and released by private citizens on their property.

19. TURKEY VULTURES: A KEEN SENSE OF SMELL

A member of the condor family, Turkey Vultures play a vital role in the environment. You will see large vultures all summer in Michigan, soaring for hours and scanning for carrion. Despite what you see in the movies, vultures generally only search for creatures that are already dead, and they don't have a voice. Hissing and puffing are the only sounds they can make. Their diets help to limit the spread of bacteria and diseases such as anthrax, rabies, and cholera. When vultures are not present in an ecosystem to clean up carcasses, it increases the numbers of undesired scavengers: rats, flies, and feral pigs.

Turkey Vultures are well adapted to their diets. Their bald or nearly bald heads are easier to keep clean and they have an extremely corrosive stomach acid that allows them to consume rotting animal flesh. The Turkey Vulture has excellent eyesight and an acute sense of smell.

Whether birds can smell at all has been discussed, argued, and researched for over 100 years. Early on, John James Audubon conducted an experiment in 1830 on Turkey Vultures, using a hidden hog carcass. Because the vultures did not feed on it, he concluded that they couldn't smell or didn't use it to hunt.

Ornithologist Kenneth Stager repeated Audubon's test in 1960 and showed that Turkey Vultures prefer fresher carcasses—typically no more than four days old—to putrid ones like Audubon hid. He even identified the specific chemical that draws vultures, when natural gas pipeliners told him they followed the birds to pipeline leaks. Decomposing carcasses give off ethyl mercaptan, the very same chemical added to natural gas to warm humans in case of a leak.

These birds are hard to miss. Turkey Vultures are two feet or taller, with a wingspan of 5-6 feet. It is all blackish-brown with a long, rounded tail, a small, featherless red head, and a short hooked bill. Males and females look alike; the female is slightly larger.

Turkey Vultures have learned to patrol the highways looking for roadkill; it's the place most people get a glimpse of this important scavenger.

20. THE BEAUTIFUL WILD TURKEY

Wild Turkeys are found in all 68 counties of the Lower Peninsula of Michigan and most counties in the Upper Peninsula. A flock of 5 to 50 birds (called a "rafter") might be living in the woods, a residential neighborhood, or even an industrial park. They require secure, elevated roosts at night, usually in tall hardwood trees. Flocks of either females or males are a common sight in the spring or fall in farm fields or open grasslands. Turkeys also enjoy visiting backyard bird feeders.

During the summer months, rafters of females can be seen encouraging their combined broods across the road. Although they look ungainly and almost prehistoric, running on the ground, turkeys are strong fliers. With excellent vision, Wild Turkeys can see in full color, and they have a periscopic vision, allowing them to see objects that are not in their direct line of sight. A turkey's field of vision is 270 degrees, compared to only 180 degrees in humans.

Wild Turkeys are big; males weigh up to 24 pounds and stand 3 feet tall. Females are smaller. They are heavily ornamented with a colorful bare head. Male turkeys (and some females) have a "beard" of specialized feathers called filoplumes, which hang down from the chest and grow longer as they mature. Some male turkeys may have two or more beards.

Although they appear to be covered in brownish feathers, when observed through binoculars, the beautiful iridescence of their feathers can be appreciated. They light up in the sunshine, revealing greens, gold, red, and bronze hues, and are one of the most colorful birds in Michigan. Wild Turkey feathers contain compartments that can either be hollow or contain color pigments. The compartments pack together into unique nanostructured arrangements to produce iridescent colors.

In addition to gobbling (which "jake" or tom turkeys do to attract a mate), you can hear turkeys make 8 different sounds. They yelp and cluck to let other hens or toms know they are in the area. Putting and clucking are sounds of alarm or when a hen is riled up. They might purr with content about a good feed or cackle in the morning when they first fly down from their roost. Young turkeys in distress run away with a "pee-pee-pee" sound. If you hear any of these sounds, look around for a chance to observe the largest game bird in the US.

Wild Turkeys made a strong comeback in Michigan, where their population was nearly decimated by hunting in the 1800s. Today, Michigan's Wild Turkeys are descendants of birds trapped in Iowa, Missouri, and Pennsylvania; a concerted effort starting in 1983 really helped rebuild the population.

21. SNOWY OWL WINTER "IRRUPTIONS"

Snowy Owls live and breed in the arctic tundra of Canada, but some owls, especially younger ones, migrate south for the winter. Their southern range extends down to southern Michigan. Look for them in the Upper and northern Lower Peninsulas, in places that mimic the Arctic tundra, such as the shorelines of Lakes Huron or Michigan, open farm fields, marshes, beaches, dunes, and even airports.

Winter is the prime time for a Snowy Owl sighting in Michigan. Snowy Owl migration patterns, breeding seasons, and the stark winter fields lure them south from Canada and the Arctic. We anticipate the return of these owls to Michigan. The large white and brown-flecked birds with piercing yellow eyes hunt in the day or night, making them easier to spot than most other owls. These are one of the largest North American owls, standing 2 feet high and with a wingspan of up to 5 feet. Females are larger than males.

Some years bring larger numbers of Snowy Owls to Michigan. Owls and other arctic birds may exhibit a short-distance migration behavior scientists call "irruptions" or invasions. Snowy Owl irruptions occur every four to five years, and it's not hunger that produces these flights, but an abundance of food during the summer breeding season. High populations of lemmings, voles, ptarmigans, and other prey (in their breeding grounds in the Arctic) lead to larger families and high numbers of young owls who are more inclined to migrate south.

Snowy Owls, coming down from the Arctic, can be remarkably approachable, especially young birds, because they are so naive around humans. It's easy for birders, photographers, and the public to approach them too closely. Snowy Owl etiquette is important; be sure to observe them from 100 yards or more and be careful not to chase them. Your car makes a great (and warm) blind for observing them from a safe distance.

22. SANDHILL CRANES ARE THE OLDEST LIVING BIRDS ON THE PLANET

Sandhill Cranes are majestic birds and the largest birds in Michigan. They stand 3 to 4 feet tall and have a wingspan of 6 feet. If your paths cross, you will surely notice them. They are gray to brown but look out for their very distinctive bright red cap. Each fall in their breeding areas, Sandhill Cranes "stage" by the thousands for migration back to their winter feeding grounds in Texas, Mexico, and other southern states. But if they have a good source of food, water, and shelter, some Sandhill Cranes remain over the winter in Michigan.

Sandhill Cranes create some spectacular opportunities for viewing in the southern part of Michigan. Near Jackson and Bellevue there are Audubon Sanctuaries where you can see the flocks stop for the night to rest. The Phyllis Haehnle Memorial Audubon Sanctuary near Waterloo Recreation Area in Jackson County is the largest roosting area for the cranes. We see them every year in the fields around Bath, and last year two of them appeared in our backyard in central Michigan. They are easy to spot in farm fields in spring.

Sandhill Cranes have a specialized coiled throat which creates their very, very loud bugling call. It's not like any other bird. When flying, cranes extend their necks, and this is one good way to tell the difference between Sandhill Cranes and Great Blue Herons in flight.

Sandhill Crane pairs build a nest in fields or marshes and raise one or two young birds a season. The nest may or may not be in the water and cranes often return to the same nest area year after year. Hatchlings leave the nest the day after they hatch and follow their parents, learning to feed themselves. They remain with them through the migration.

Sandhill Cranes may stay with the same mate for many years. In the spring, cranes perform elaborate courtship dances where they twirl and bounce and throw their necks back to attract or re-engage with their mates.

23. AMERICAN KESTRELS BENEFIT MICHIGAN'S FRUIT INDUSTRY

The microclimate in some areas of Michigan creates the perfect environment for fruit growers. Cherry farmers in northern Michigan make this state the cherry capital of the world. The southwest side of Michigan has many fruit orchards, and Michigan apples are grown everywhere in the Lower Peninsula.

Biologists encourage Michigan fruit farmers to add nest boxes for North America's smallest raptor, the American Kestrel. American Kestrels hunt small rodents and fruit-eating birds, and their presence alone in an orchard can significantly reduce these costly pests. Fruit-eating birds avoid orchards entirely if they see kestrels. Cherry growers in Leelanau County have a history of setting up nest boxes for kestrels, putting them on telephone poles that hawks often choose as their perches. The American Kestrel has been called the sparrow hawk.

American Kestrels are falcons, America's smallest falcon. These daytime-hunting raptors are fast flyers and make high-speed dives to catch prey. Catch a glimpse of one perched, and you can see they are russet-colored on the back to the tail, with a black band near the tip of that tail. They have a double stripe of black on their white faces. Males have gray-blue wings. If you see them in flight, they are very light-colored underneath.

Starting in September, people gather in the Detroit River area, to be close to the narrow 4 mile stretch of open water where 1000s of migrating raptors from Canada cross each fall. Exciting counts of American Kestrels cross at Lake Erie Metropark and Pointe Mouillee State Game Area in southeast Michigan. This is an excellent opportunity to see Osprey, Sharp-shinned Hawks, Broad-winged Hawks, Swainson's Hawks, and Bald Eagles. The migration continues with different birds through November.

24. LIFE-OR-DEATH STRUGGLES OF AN EASTERN TOWHEE

When I started to write *50 Things to Know About Birds in Michigan*, I asked my husband David, an avid birder his entire life, for one of his most memorable bird stories. He described a battle he witnessed in a southwest Michigan apple orchard between three Eastern Towhees and a rat snake. A male and female towhee were locked in battle with the snake over a fledgling. Eastern Towhees are birds of the open woods and brushy areas, and they nest on the ground. Snakes are a serious predator to ground-nesting birds. Both adults pecked and drew snake blood; it was a life-or-death struggle. Eventually, human intervention drove it off.

The Eastern Towhee is commonly known as "Chewink", after the sound of its call. It sounds a bit like "drink your teeee." It's smaller and more slender than a robin. It has distinctive bold black and reddish-brown markings. The head and back are jet black, the belly is white, and it has robin-red patches on its sides. The wings show some white barring and the eyes are usually red. Its longish tail is held upright as it forages in dense leaf over. You may hear it scratching before you see it.

Towhees are solitary birds; male towhees may defend territories many times larger than needed to provide food. They forage using the double-footed, backward hop to scratch and reveal what's just below the leaf litter's surface.

Until 1995, the Spotted Towhee and the Eastern Towhee were considered variants of the same species, the Rufous-sided Towhee. Each is now considered to be a unique species.

BIRDS OF THE WOODLANDS

25. RAIN CROWS: THE YELLOW-BILLED CUCKOO

The Yellow-billed Cuckoo relies on obscurity for survival. Cuckoo birds shyly inhabit dense leafy trees and thickets during the summer here in Michigan. Listen for their stuttering, harsh, "ka-ka-ka-ka-kow-kowp", it may be your only clue. Imagining that it sings for rain on dark cloudy days in spring and early summer, people have called this bird the rain crow.

You might see Yellow-billed Cuckoos feasting on hairy tent caterpillars; they often forage on their tent-like nests. Even caterpillar-eating birds shun these caterpillars, which are highly destructive to deciduous trees. Yellow-billed Cuckoos have a well-evolved strategy for eating them. They pull a caterpillar from its tent and roll it back and forth in their bill, taking off many of the irritating hairs. Some of the hair remains and ends up in their stomachs. Inevitably, hair builds up and prevents digestion, and the entire stomach lining is cast off and purged. That behavior reminds us of the cat!

Yellow-billed Cuckoos are about seven inches long, slim birds with a long tail, brown above, white on the belly, and rusty patches on their wings. Catching a glimpse from below, you can see large white spots on a black tail. Yellow-billed Cuckoos have a strong bill; it is black on top and yellow on the bottom. To compare, they are about the size of a Blue Jay, and males and females look similar.

The male courtship feeds the female, and they build a flimsy saucer of twigs in bushes or small saplings. Eggs are incubated by both sexes. Cuckoos occasionally lay their eggs in another cuckoo's nest and rarely in the nests of other bird species, but they are not serious brood parasites like cowbirds.

We welcome these birds to Michigan, especially in central and southern Michigan. Our forests are susceptible to Lymantria dispar, or the gypsy moth. Yellow-billed Cuckoos eat these caterpillars and are crucial for controlling this pest.

26. VIREOS HEARD HERE

Vireos are well-camouflaged birds with colorful songs described as melodious, cheerful, repetitive, and unstoppable. A vireo male sings his high-pitched notes on constant replay. Six vireo species stopover or summer in Michigan and the Red-eyed Vireo is one of the longest singers. You can hear him sing on hot summer afternoons, long after other birds have stopped.

Vireos tend to stay out of sight in leafy treetops. Look for a blue-gray crown, white eyebrows bordered above and below in black, dark olive back, wings, and tail, with a white underside. With binoculars, you can see the Red-eyed Vireo's red eyes. They resemble warblers, but they are larger and have heavier bills.

Red-eyed Vireos need deciduous or mixed forests with a dense canopy cover to breed, often near rivers or streams. You may find them in forested city parks, cemeteries with old-growth trees, and orchards. They feed on all types of insects and caterpillars, and the later summer berries. The females build a dainty nest cup with the rim woven into a forked twig, a well-constructed build.

Male Red-eyed Vireos spend their energy establishing suitable nesting territories and frequently engage in chases and aggression to defend them, and they sing their heads off.

27. SCARLET TANAGERS - THE OTHER RED BIRD

When I was young, we had a picture book and in it was a picture of a Scarlet Tanager. It looked so exotic and when I finally saw one here in Michigan, I was especially excited and it was just as spectacular as the picture. Males in the summer breeding season are brilliant red with black wings. Females are somewhat smaller and greenish-yellow, with darker wings. Females blend exceptionally well with the trees and can be difficult to spot. Both sexes are stout birds with a short pointed bill.

Tanagers are tropical birds who winter in the rain forests of the lowlands east of the Andes mountains. That they find their way to Michigan to breed in the summer is a real treat. They tend to remain high in leafy treetops where they glean insects and berries. Sometimes they "hawk" or catch insects in mid-air like flycatchers. We see them almost every year when they visit our juneberry trees. A late freeze in spring can sometimes force them into the open, searching for insects along roadsides or in gardens. They occasionally appear where there have been extensive plantings of shade trees in suburban areas, parks, and cemeteries. Tanagers need a large patch of forest, several acres to be successful. They spend most of their time high in the canopy, which makes them more difficult to spot.

In the spring, male Scarlet Tanagers arrive and establish breeding territories before the females' return. Males attract a mate with vocalizations, and he displays for the female. He spreads his wings and stretches out his neck to show off his bright scarlet back. Both male and female tanagers are aggressive towards other birds who approach their nests. Male Tanagers have even been seen chasing females back to their nests.

28. RUBY-CROWNED KINGLETS ARE EXCITABLE BIRDS

Ruby-crowned Kinglets are tiny, plump songbirds. Among North American birds, only hummingbirds are smaller. They spend summer high in the tall evergreen forests of the Upper Peninsula and Canada, but we see them during spring and fall migrations, darting around in the low woods and thickets. In October, they fly south to the southern United States and Mexico.

Ruby-crowned Kinglets are often recognized by their behavior. It's a nervous bird; it flicks its wings nervously, and if startled or excited, the Ruby-crowned Kinglet will raise his mohawk of red feathers. It is otherwise inconspicuous, with a grayish-olive body above and two white wing bars. Its song is loud and out of proportion for this bird, described as a distinctive song that builds to an incredibly loud ending.

Kinglets have large clutch sizes compared to other birds, maybe 10 - 12 eggs. That represents up to 80% of the mass of the female. Thankfully, both sexes share in feeding and raising the chicks.

Ruby-crowned Kinglets often forage by hovering to reach the undersides of branches. During migration, they join mixed-species flocks of wood warblers, chickadees, and the usual visitors to bird feeders in central and southern Michigan.

They migrate at night, so look for them in the morning.

29. RED-SHOULDERED HAWKS - KEE-YAH, KEE-YAH!

A Red-shouldered Hawk regularly perches above our bird feeder. It's all about the food chain; he is there looking for the mice, voles and other small animals inevitably attracted to the feeder. The other birds (Black-capped Chickadees, Nuthatches, titmice, and various woodpeckers) bravely continue to forage. These hawks may live all

65

year in Michigan, more commonly in southern Michigan in the winter, and in northern Michigan to breed in the summer. They prefer mature, forested floodplain habitats. Look for them along the Manistee River in west-central Michigan, near Lake Michigan.

Red-shouldered Hawks are raptors (birds of prey), named for the rusty-red patches on their shoulders. Their chests have rich orange barring and on the back, it looks like a soft brown and white checkerboard pattern. It has a heavily banded tail. They are large birds, 24 inches tall, but just medium-sized compared to other hawks. Many hawks can be difficult to distinguish. Their markings are similar, and from a distance, it can be difficult to tell them apart. Even for experienced birders, identities are pieced together from multiple clues that point to one species over another.

If you see them perched, one way to identify hawks is by the length of their wings, compared to their tail. Red-shouldered Hawks are buteos, the group of hawks distinguished by long, broad wings. When perched, the ends of the wings are about as long as the tail. They stay perched for long periods, to await prey. The other group of hawks is accipiters, distinguished by short, broad wings and adapted for fast flight in wooded country.

Red-shouldered Hawks have the loudest calls, and could just be the noisiest of all the raptors. You might hear their high-pitched "Kee-yah, Kee-yah" calls while they are perched close or flying overhead.

30. PROTHONOTARY WARBLERS ARE NOT A CONFUSING BIRD

The Peterson Field Guide to Eastern Birds has a section titled "Confusing Fall Warblers", and when we were young my brother and I got the biggest kick from that description. Whenever we saw a bird we could not identify, we would call it a "confusing warbler!" Warbler identification can be quite difficult and there are entire books on the subject, but there are some warblers in Michigan we can usually see, and identification is easy; the Prothonotary Warbler is one of them.

Prothonotary Warblers have some unique characteristics that help identify them. They are bright golden yellow on the head, breast, and underside, with an olive-green back and gray wings. Males are more vivid and have a darker bill than females. Their bright yellow color is quite striking, and they are nicknamed the "Golden Swamp Warbler." The Prothonotary Warbler got its name from the bright yellow robes worn by Roman Catholic papal clerks, known as prothonotaries.

They are one of two warblers in North America that nest in tree cavities (like old woodpecker holes) and the only one in Michigan. Prothonotary Warblers are also one of a few warblers who will accept a birdhouse. They inhabit bottomland forest wetlands throughout central and southern Michigan, the northern edge of their summer homes. They migrate early in the autumn and return in April.

The Maple River State Game Area is one place we like to see the Prothonotary Warbler. It's mid-Michigan's largest contiguous wetland complex, an area of floodplains, lowlands, and marshes along the Maple River that begins in Gratiot County and extends into Clinton County. There is an easy access road off of US-27 where the road passes over the wildlife flooding area and a short hike from there to a viewing tower.

31. PILEATED WOODPECKERS - THE REAL WOODY WOODPECKER

The largest woodpecker in North America is the Pileated Woodpecker, and it's a sight - a large mostly black bird with a shockingly red head crest, white stripes on the face and neck, and a prominent chisel-shaped bill. About the size of a crow, they may take you by surprise when they land and grip the side of a tree in woodlots, the forest edge, and even in city parks across Michigan. Males have a noticeable patch of red feathers on their faces and both males and females have wingspans of up to 30 inches. Its unique look and size make it easy to identify. Pileated Woodpeckers can be recognized by their undulating flight patterns, when you can see the flash of their white wing patches.

Pileated Woodpeckers were the model for the irritating cartoon character Woody Woodpecker and his manic 5-note "hah-hah-hah-hah-hah " laugh. Real Pileated Woodpeckers are quite vocal, with a high, clear, series of rattling sounds. Fledgling Pileated

Woodpeckers are quite raucous and keep both parents more than busy looking for carpenter ants, termites, beetles, and other insects from excavated holes they make in dead timber. Mature forests and trees are very important for supporting woodpeckers. You can spot their activity in the woods - large excavations in deadwood with lots of chips below.

Both male and female Pileated Woodpeckers drum powerfully on trees; it's a sound once heard you will not forget, a fairly slow, deep pounding noise that lasts about 3 seconds. Males drum in late winter to establish and defend a territory; they don't migrate. When the leaves are off the trees in the winter, it's an excellent time to spot them in the woods.

Pileateds are highly territorial and a monogamous pair inhabits and defends their territory all year round. Both drum as part of courtship rituals, and either sex may drum to call to a mate, or in response to an intruder.

Their nest is a deep cavity excavated or naturally occurring in a tree. It can take up to a month to construct. These nests are seldom used for a second year and that makes for great housing opportunities for Screech Owls, Black-capped Chickadees, Wood Ducks, bats, and other species of woodpeckers.

32. OVENBIRDS ARE NAMED FOR THEIR NESTS

Look down in the shady woods to see this unique wood warbler working the forest floor. The Ovenbird's habitat can make it difficult to see, but its loud, ringing "teacher, teacher, teacher" call is distinct. Territorial male Ovenbirds sing at night during spring and summer

The term "ovenbird" is a reference to this bird's nest, which is a domed structure made of grass and usually on the ground. The entrance on the side, like an old-fashioned, Dutch oven, is where the name comes from. Ovenbird is a term used for many birds in this family who also build a domed nest with a side entrance.

Ovenbirds prefer the ground in leafy woods, thickets, or undergrowth. They need large areas of mature hardwoods or mixed forests to successfully breed. If you are lucky enough to see them on the ground, they remind you of a chicken, taking a few steps, pausing, turning their head to look at the ground before moving on.

71

Ovenbirds are not flashy birds; they are brownish to olive on top, with bold black spotting on the underparts aligned into rows. They have a white eye-ring, and a black-edged orange crown; the bird looks like a small thrush. Males and females are similar.

Most wood warblers hop on the ground, but the Ovenbird walks deliberately, with his tail cocked up; that is one way you can identify them and distinguish them from thrushes, which look similar.

33. NORTHERN FLICKERS HAVE THE LONGEST TONGUES

Northern Flickers are members of the woodpecker family, but you are more likely to find them on the ground and not perched on the side of a tree. Ants are a big part of their diet, so they spend much of their time foraging on the ground, using their exceptionally long tongues to probe anthills. Northern Flickers have the longest tongue of any woodpecker (in North America.) They can extend it two inches past the end of their bills, and it's sticky and perfectly adapted for retrieving ants.

Northern Flickers drum on objects to communicate and defend their territory, like all woodpeckers. The extra-long woodpecker's tongue is so long that it wraps around the back of its skull and this adaptation helps to protect the woodpecker's brain when they are banging their bills against a hard object. The tongue compresses the head and holds the brain like a seatbelt.

Northern Flickers are the only brown woodpecker. It is a large bird, 10-14 inches long. The brown back and wings are barred with black, and the tan breast has black spots and a wide black band. There are several subspecies of Northern Flickers. In Michigan, we have the yellow-shafted or eastern Northern Flickers. These males have a heart-shaped red spot on the back of their head and when they fly you can see the underside of the wings appear yellow.

Flickers are a great bird to observe because it spends so much time on the ground and it's large enough to see their beautiful markings, without binoculars.

34. LISTEN FOR RUFFED GROUSE DRUMMING

My first encounter with a wild Ruffed Grouse was finding one perched in the trees above my bird feeder. It looked a bit out of place, like a barnyard chicken in a tree. Ruffed Grouse are patterned with dark brown bars or spots on a rusty-brown or gray background. The tail is barred, with a wide, black band near the tip. On their heads is a slight crest of fan-shaped feathers.

Ruffed Grouse live in woodlands from Alaska to Georgia. Michigan is an important portion of their habitat. Grouse thrive best in young, aspen forests, oak forests, and lowland brush. Ruffed Grouse visit bird feeders in neighborhoods where natural habitat is available. Where they are not hunted, grouse are very tolerant of humans.

Adult male grouse establish core territories and aggressively defend them against other males during the breeding season. Males select a stone, log, or mound of earth from which they perform a display called "drumming." Grouse drum to warn other males and attract hens. Grouse beat their wings to create a putt-putt-putt sound similar to a small gasoline engine. Drumming goes on all year, but you are most likely to hear it in spring.

Females may visit the territory of multiple males, but they raise their young alone. Hens hollow out a depression in the leaf litter at the base of a tree or stump and lay one egg a day until she has eight to 14 light-colored eggs. After the last egg is laid, she incubates the nest. Soon after hatching, the chicks follow the hen to a summer range of young hardwood trees.

Forest management and the desire by the public to stop cutting trees on public land have significantly reduced Ruffed Grouse populations. Grouse need young trees to thrive.

35. LIKE A SLIDE WHISTLE - BABY BARRED OWLS

The thing about bird feeders is that you are not only feeding the birds (or the obvious squirrels!) You are witnessing an entire food chain, one which runs all day and all night. We have seen foxes move into our yard where a bird feeder was located and used year-round. Seeds attract smaller critters: mice, voles, weasels - which in turn attract the top of the food chain, the Barred Owl.

Barred Owls (not to be confused with Barn Owls) are one of the most common Michigan owls. Their name comes from their brown barred markings, although let's face it, it can be difficult to observe these nocturnal birds. They are up to 2 feet tall with wingspans of 4 feet, and they fly silently through the woods on their specially evolved feathers. Luckily, they are very curious, so once disturbed they may only fly a few feet away to perch again.

Barred Owls favor woodlands, wooded river bottoms, and wooded swamps. Even if you don't observe them, Barred Owls have a rich and wonderful vocabulary of hooting sounds, the classic owl hooting you associate with scary movies or Halloween sounds. The call is described as 8 or 9 notes roughly in the cadence "Who cooks for you" but it is wildly richer. I have heard hooting duets which are downright spectacular.

But it's the baby Barred Owls which have the most peculiar call, one I hope you have the chance to hear. They use that call to keep track of their parents' location when they are left alone. Like a reedy slide whistle, baby owls have an unmistakable sound, giving away their location. In the early midsummer evenings, we hear them in our backyard.

Still widespread and common in Michigan, Barred Owls are permanent residents in the woods throughout Michigan. Listen for their spooky calls at dusk or dawn.

36. KIRTLAND'S WARBLER

Whether you are a birder, hope to be one, or, just want to see one of these rarest songbirds, look for a Kirtland's Warbler tour if you are near Grayling or Roscommon, in north-central Michigan. It is the best way to ensure you are looking in just the right stands of jack pines, just the right size and age for Kirtland's Warblers.

Kirtland's Warblers were nearly extinct in the 1900s as the exact size and age of these trees used for breeding was disappearing. Kirtland's warblers nest in a single area in north-central Michigan. And the crucial jack pines require fire to release their seeds from the cone; control of forest fires in Michigan had a drastic, negative impact on these unique warblers.

If you are lucky to see one, they are a relatively large warbler, blue-gray above and yellow below, with strongly black-striped backs. They have a white eye-ring and two whitish wing bars. Females look similar but a bit darker. They forage close to the ground and characteristically wag their tails up and down.

Males arrive in early May from the Bahamas to a loose colony and begin to defend a territory.

They need territory; a pair of Kirtland's Warblers require at least eight acres of dense young jack pine forest to build a nest, which they build on the ground underneath the lowest pine branches. Until they depart in August to October, they forage for insects, eat pine sap and wild blueberries (a Michigan treat!)

Biologists didn't discover where these warblers bred until 1903, and then decades later realized their decline was related to the lack of young jack pines and parasitic cowbirds, which lay their eggs in other bird's nests. Controlled burning to mimic the natural jack pine cycle is a tempting solution, but instead, jack pine trees are cut and seedlings replanted on large tracts of land in their breeding area. An aggressive program of removing cowbird eggs from their nests (thankfully on the ground) has created a stable and growing population on their traditional breeding grounds. Nearby state parks know exactly where the best spots are to quietly observe this iconic Michigan warbler.

37. INDIGO BUNTING, THE BLUEST OF THE "BLUE" BIRDS

There are several "blue" birds in Michigan: the Great Blue Heron, the Blue Jay, Kingfishers, and the Bluebird, but none are as shockingly blue as the Indigo Bunting. Hopping from branch to branch through the bushy brush, along roads, rivers, or woodland edges, the Indigo Bunting male is brilliant blue. The female in her soft brown feathers is much more difficult to spot. Indigo Buntings will use small birdhouses or visit nyger thistle seed-stocked feeders, and they are not rare in suburban areas; you might see them during their spring or fall migration through Michigan.

Indigo Bunting, nicknamed "Blue Canaries" are members of the Cardinalidae family, where the males are brightly colored and females have more subtle hues. This is called sexual dimorphism and it's a general trait of Cardinalidaes. The blue color of the male Indigo Bunting's feathers is due to their microscopic structures, which refract, scatter, and reflect blue light. It's the same mechanism that makes the sky appear blue. There is no blue pigment; the exact shade of blue you will see depends on the ambient light. In winter, when the birds migrate from Michigan to Mexico or the southern U.S., the males become browner - the true "color" of the feathers.

Buntings are small birds, the size of a small sparrow. The word bunting is Scottish in origin and means plump. They hunt by gleaning low shrubs for insects and seeds. Bird feeders with black thistle seed have a chance to attract Indigo Buntings, but they are mostly solitary birds who feed alone. You may see the males feeding their young fledglings and teaching them to hunt while the females build a second nest during their summer season in Michigan.

Males sing all summer long to protect their territory, the best way to find one is to recognize its song, usually a series of six notes, some say it sounds as if they're singing "What, what, where, where, see it, see it." They're most vocal at dawn, when a male may repeat his song many times a minute.

38. DOWNY WOODPECKERS ARE HARDINESS, INDUSTRY, VIVACITY

The Downy Woodpecker is the smallest woodpecker in North America and a visitor everywhere in Michigan. It is common in backyard feeders, in city parks; it feels at home anywhere with deciduous trees. Its small size allows it to feed on plant stalks as well as large trees, so expect to see it in places you might not expect a woodpecker. The Downy Woodpecker is a social bird and often travels with a flock of other woodpeckers or small songbirds. Downy Woodpeckers remain in Michigan year-round.

I often misidentify the Downy Woodpecker as a Hairy Woodpecker, until I see them together. The Downy is considerably smaller and has a shorter bill than its look-alike cousin. Markings for both birds feature a distinctive zebra-like black and white pattern on their backs and wings, and white or light colors on the underside. Males have a bright red spot on the top of their heads.

John James Audubon described Downy Woodpeckers this way. "Hardiness, industry, or vivacity. If you watch its motions, you will find it ever at work." They climb acrobatically on tree trunks and stems to excavate cavities and glean insects with their long, specialized tongues.

All woodpeckers have adapted in several ways which make their unique "drumming" behavior possible. Special adaptations allow woodpeckers to make their iconic hammer sounds without injury. Their long tongues wrap around the back of their heads to protect their brains, and their skull bones are sponge-like and absorb shocks. Even the eyes are adapted; they have a clear membrane that slips over the eye and helps hold it tightly in place.

In May the Downy Woodpeckers look for the perfect spot for a nest. They excavate an entrance, a perfect circle large enough for just one to come in or out at a time. To prevent detection, they carry out the wood chips and disperse them far away from the nest. They often choose holes where lichen or fungus covers the entrance. Both parents raise a single brood each summer.

39. CAROLINA WRENS SING DUETS IN SOUTHERN MICHIGAN

Carolina Wrens are moving back into southern Michigan after deep winter snows in the 1970s pushed them out. Wrens are not colorful birds but they have beautiful songs. Look for them in shrubby places that provide these shy birds' cover. Carolina Wrens are reddish-brown birds with a distinct white throat and eye line. Their wings and long tails have fine black barring, and their bill is long and thin. Both males and females appear similar. They are similar in size to Northern Cardinals.

Carolina Wrens sings a distinctive melody sounding like "tea kettle tea kettle tea kettle." It reminds me of the Northern Cardinal. These wrens like parks and residential areas. You can attract them to your backyard feeder with nuts or mealworms.

An odd habit of many male wrens is the building of dummy nests in their territory. Up to 20 nests that are never used have been found. They probably do this to protect their nests from parasitic birds who lay their eggs in other birds' nests, like the cowbird. Or they are targeting birds or mammals which eat eggs, hoping that after checking several empty nests the predator will leave.

Carolina Wrens are monogamous wrens who mate for life. They usually forage in pairs and will stay together in their territory year-round.

40. BALTIMORE ORIOLES EAT HAIRY CATERPILLARS AND WE LOVE THAT IN MICHIGAN

Hummingbird feeders in Michigan attract much more than the Ruby-throated Hummingbird. Baltimore Orioles, with their flaming orange bellies and rump, black head, and white wing bars, are often seen at feeders, especially in early spring. These nectar, insect, and fruit-eating birds are summer songbirds common in open woods, or groves of shady trees in town. They were named after Lord Baltimore, the first governor of Maryland, whose coat of arms share the same colors. I hear their whistling songs at my feeder, often before the hummers arrive. Look for them at the end of April.

Baltimore Orioles are icterids, a songbird family including these other birds you may see in Michigan: Red-winged Blackbirds, Cowbirds, Grackles, and Meadowlarks. All of these birds have been very successful at adapting to humans; Orioles' use of hummingbird feeders is a recently learned behavior. During their summer breeding orioles mostly eat insects. Happily for Michigan's oaks and other hardwoods, they like the hairy Lymantria dispa caterpillars (formerly called gypsy moths) avoided by many other birds. Orioles love fruit and especially the mid-summer ripening mulberry trees. Draw them to a backyard feeder with oranges, berries, or even grape jelly.

Look for Baltimore Orioles along the edges of rivers, swamps, lakeshores, open woodlands, farms, and scrublands. You won't find them in deep forests. They build unique-looking, woven, bag-shaped nests in leafy trees. Males and females, who are yellower and more mottled, raise their young together. Once out of the nest, the young are very raucous and chase their parents through the treetops, begging for fresh insects. They remain together in Michigan all summer, eventually migrating south to Mexico and South America for the winter.

41. BROWN CREEPERS ARE MASTERS OF CAMOUFLAGE

The Brown Creeper's color keeps it well camouflaged while it forages on trees. This is a tiny woodland bird with short legs and a long tail with stiffened, pointed tips. It has a thin, curved bill, perfectly evolved for gleaning and probing bark. With short legs and long toes, it moves up tree trunks similar to nuthatches, but it cannot move down the trunk. They move with short, jerky movements, using their long tails for support.

They often share trees, creepers working the bottom of the trees, and nuthatches foraging higher in the trees on smaller branches. We sometimes see them in the mixed flock of birds at the winter bird feeders, especially suet feeders. They are so small they find food overlooked by larger birds.

Their plumage matches the color and texture of the bark so well they nearly disappear when they stay still and cling to that bark.

Their white underparts are mostly hidden. They look like a piece of bark has come to life.

Brown Creepers build a unique nest. They layer silky moth cocoons and spider egg cases with twigs and strips of bark, and locate their nest behind a strip of bark hanging off a tree. Their nests are extremely difficult to see. Creepers need forests with old-growth trees with plenty of standing deadwood for nesting and foraging. Brown Creepers breed in northern Michigan and often migrate into southern Michigan during winter. They sometimes roost in groups during nonbreeding seasons to stay warm.

Brown Creepers are the only creeper in North America.

42. GREAT CRESTED FLYCATCHERS USE SNAKESKINS

Great Crested Flycatchers are birds of the dense leafy forest. It lives and forages in the tall trees in the summer in Michigan. It is much more colorful than most other flycatchers. It avoids pure conifer stands and prefers continuous deep forests, forest edges, and orchards. It's a migrator which spends winter in the tropics.

The Great Crested is a bit smaller than an American Robin but large for a flycatcher, 7 inches long. Its most striking feature is its gray bushy crest, which it doesn't always have extended. The back and wings are gray to olive, and the belly is a lemony yellow. Tails and wing tips are rufous colored. Like other tyrants, male and female Great Cresteds are similar. There are hundreds of species of flycatchers.

Vocalizations are important to flycatchers. They sing a "dawn song" before sunrise. Their most characteristic sound is a single loud "whee-eep," used to communicate between mates or parents and young birds.

The flycatcher diet is mostly insects. It hunts by flying out from a perch to take insects from foliage in trees or to catch them in midair. It usually does not feed on the ground. They also enjoy fruit and berries.

Both sexes help to build the nest; the Great Crested Flycatcher is the only eastern flycatcher that nests in holes, either a natural cavity or an old woodpecker hole. They may also use a birdhouse.

Most Great Crested Flycatchers include a piece of shed snakeskin in the nest lining and/or displayed outside their nest. Biologists theorize one reason they do this is to deter flying squirrels, which eat flycatcher eggs. Rat snakes eat flying squirrels so flycatchers (and the few other birds who use it) are using snakeskin as a deterrent. Studies show that nests with snakeskin are left alone by flying squirrels.

BIRDS OF THE SUBURBS AND BACKYARDS

43. AMERICAN ROBIN THE OFFICIAL STATE BIRD OF MICHIGAN

In 1931 the American Robin was selected as the state bird of Michigan after a contest by the Michigan Audubon Society. It beat the Black-capped Chickadee.

This very common songbird is a member of the thrush family, and like other thrushes, it's a strong and melodic singer. American Robin is one of the first birds we look for in spring, but not all robins migrate. Some form large flocks and remain together during the fall and winter. In the spring, when we see our first American Robin, we always see many of the males together. They arrive first to claim territory by singing or even fighting. Several male robins chase and pursue a single female until she makes her selection.

Male robins have rust or russet-colored feathers on their chest, a black head, white outlines around their eyes, and a yellow bill. They have gray wings and backs. Female robins look similar to males, but their colors are much duller and sometimes they can be difficult to identify.

These prolific breeders can raise 2 or 3 broods a year. They are not picky about nesting near humans and seem to have made their peace with us. Females do most of the work to build a nest which is familiar to all of us using sticks anchored into a mud foundation. Pale blue "robin egg blue" eggs are tended by the female and after hatching, both parents feed and raise the young. Once they leave the nest, males may tend the young while the female returns to the nest to begin another brood.

Brown-headed Cowbirds are parasitic birds who lay their speckled eggs among the robin's eggs. But robins are efficient at recognizing and removing these unwanted eggs from the nest before they hatch and compete with their own chicks. Robins may be able to see a wider spectrum of colors than humans, making it easier to discern the interloper's eggs.

American Robins were named by early American settlers who thought the birds resembled the unrelated European Robin or "robin redbreast."

44. LOOK DOWN FOR DARK-EYED JUNCOS

Dark-eyed Juncos are a sign of winter in Michigan. These slate-colored birds are seen only in the winter months. Juncos migrate south for the winter months, and lower Michigan is their "south." Juncos live in pine and deciduous forests. In winter, they flock to birdfeeders, where juncos will prefer millet seed, which many other birds tend to ignore.

Easy to recognize without binoculars; Dark-eyed Juncos are medium-size sparrows with a round head, long tail, and a small, pinkish bill. They are dark gray, with a grayish-white belly. You will notice that their heads are very dark. Females are a bit browner. Nothing else you see in the winter feeder looks like a junco, and they will be the birds scavenging seeds that have fallen to the ground. Juncos enforce a pecking order. Males juncos are dominant over females, and adults are dominant over juveniles. Dominant birds peck at other birds to chase them away.

Dark-eyed Juncos sometimes "ride" a grass or weed stem. They land on a seed cluster and let their weight ride it to the ground, where their weight holds the stem and allows the bird to pick off the seeds. Juncos look for food close to ground cover, and they forage in flocks, both strategies to protect them from predators. Dark-eyed Juncos tend to migrate to the same area every year. The flock will stay in an area of around 10 acres.

See a winter feeder? Look down for the juncos.

45. I'M "CONFIDING" WITH YOU - I LOVE BLACK-CAPPED CHICKADEES

These sturdy, energetic and fearless woodland songbirds can be seen everywhere in Michigan where they are anything but common. Their behavior and antics at the bird feeder are enjoyable any time of the year. And in Michigan, feeders are everywhere and not limited to the backyard. Restaurants, Dr. offices, ski resorts, cabins to lakefronts, anyplace a few birds gather for seeds, the chickadee is often the leader of roving flocks of titmice, creepers, nuthatches, and other birds searching for food. Black-capped Chickadees live in wooded and suburban areas everywhere in Michigan, where they are (mostly) permanent residents.

They are small birds and easy to identify by the black cap and throat patch, which meet at their short, pointed bill to highlight a bright white triangle across the face. Even before you see them, you will certainly hear their cheery-sounding "chick-a-dee-dee-dee" call.

Chickadees spend the winters in these mixed flock groups but toward the end of winter, they pair off to defend territory and build a nest in a hole in a tree - sometimes an old woodpecker hole or other crevice they can hollow out. They are monogamous and mate for life. You may be lucky to see the male doing some ritual feeding of the female during courting. After the eggs are laid it's the female who exclusively sits her nest. Both sexes help to raise their offspring which are ready to leave the nest in a bit more than 2 weeks.

Members of the family paridae, chickadees eat both insects and seeds. At the feeder, their behavior is particularly interesting to watch. Although they travel in groups, a single chickadee will fly into the feeder, choose their plump seed, and immediately fly away to either eat or hide that seed. They anchor food with their tiny feet and use the pointed bill to hammer them open. Chickadees are "confiding" birds and may even be persuaded to take food directly from a human, with a bit of patience. Confiding is a birding term meaning that a bird will allow a close approach of humans.

In addition to all those black oil sunflower seeds in your bird feeder, chickadees eat small insects, spiders, and spider eggs. Working in the trees, they use their pointed beaks to explore bark crevices or perform more acrobatic moves working upside down at the tip of branches, courtesy of their extremely strong legs. The seeds they don't immediately consume are hidden in caches and retrieved weeks or months later, a feat involving a large spatial memory.

Chickadees are welcomed by other birds to feeders and food sources. They don't sit by idly when predators approach, chickadees participate in "mobbing", where birds chase, attack, surround, dive bomb, or vigorously scold a predator. Chickadees find a nearby perch and scold owls, hawks, snakes, cats, or any other interloper. They are bold and inquisitive.

46. CHIPPING SPARROWS WANT YOUR HAIR

Chipping Sparrows are tiny birds who have adapted very well to the short grass and shrubbery of suburban landscapes, and you might see them anywhere in Michigan. Originally a bird of the open pine woods, "chippies" now weave their nests in parks or gardens from grass and twigs, and then line it with animal hair. At one time when America was more rural, Chipping Sparrows used mostly horsehair; today you can help them out by putting some hair from a dog or cat grooming on your lawn in the springtime.

Feeding mostly on the ground, like little chickens, chipping sparrows are fairly easy to identify by their behavior and small size. Look for a rufous or rusty red crown of feathers on the top of their heads, a white face, and a black line through the eye. Their conical bills are perfect for husking seeds. Males and females look alike. In Michigan, we see the Eastern Chipping Sparrow. They lose their colorful breeding cap a bit when fall comes and they flock up for their migration south to the southern US, Mexico, and Central America.

Chipping sparrows often raise two broods per year and the male may have more than one mate. Both sexes feed their young caterpillars and insects. Adults pare down larger insects like grasshoppers, removing their legs before feeding them to the nestlings.

At the bird feeder, Chippies cannot open larger seeds and prefer millet instead. On the ground, you can see Chipping Sparrows foraging using the "double-scratch" behavior. The bird jumps quickly forward and back, two times. Each forward jump lightly scratches the leaf litter with both feet, and the return jump pulls the litter aside to expose the tasty morsels underneath.

They are fun to watch and somewhat confiding, which means they tolerate humans nearby.

47. RUBY-THROATED HUMMINGBIRDS ARE FIERCE AND ENTERTAINING

Ruby-throated Hummingbirds entertain us every summer with acrobatic territorial displays and intense, brief skirmishes with other males. Males arrive in spring to select around one-quarter of an acre of nectar-bearing flowers or one with a hummingbird feeder. They drive off all males and non-mating females. Males don't defend a nest; they defend a food source – with gusto! To woo females, male Ruby-throated Hummingbirds make giant u-shaped flights. These arcs reach 20 to 30 feet and are accompanied by a whirring sound.

When the breeding season is over, the males become less aggressive; or they are simply outnumbered by females and juvenile hummingbirds. That is when stage two of the hummingbird entertainment starts. Seven to ten hummingbirds carefully monitoring each other and sharing four feeding stations makes me dizzy to watch, but I love it.

Occasionally, other hummingbird species are seen in Michigan, but the Ruby-throated Hummingbird is the only regular visitor to upper and lower Michigan. Look for them in flower gardens with red-colored flowers and at nectar feeders. Hummingbirds are not the only birds that eat nectar. Orioles, woodpeckers, and sapsuckers also visit feeders.

Ruby-throated hummingbirds are iridescent green on the head and back, with light underparts. Males have a brilliant ruby-red patch of feathers on their throat which glows in the sunlight.

Ornithologists have tested how hummingbirds use the color red to find nectar, and they discovered that it's just a guide. Switching the color of "flowers" did not confuse the hummingbirds, who visited the flowers with the most nectar, regardless of its color.

48. NUTHATCHES: THE UPSIDE DOWN BIRDS

Red-breasted and White-breasted Nuthatches are well known for their foraging style. In addition to foraging while walking up tree trunks, these little birds commonly forage while walking down the trunk, facing down. Not many birds can accomplish this feat and in North America, no other bird walks down trees. That makes it easy to spot a nuthatch. They flock during the winter with chickadees, titmice, and other winter birdfeeder visitors.

Nuthatches are predominately gray and white or grey and reddish. They are short and squat, sometimes looking awkward walking flat on the ground. Their heads are black on the top with a white band through the eye. They are not related to woodpeckers but nuthatches also work up and down tree trunks, gleaning insects from bark. Nuthatches brace themselves to trees with the help of their tail feathers.

Technically nuthatches are not walking down the bark, they are jumping from foothold to foothold, and holding on with their strong toes and legs. Nuthatches have four toes, with three of them facing forward and one backward. This backward-facing toe, shaped like a claw that curves downwards, is called the hallux. Biologists think that nuthatches walk down trees to see a different perspective and find insects not seen by other birds. This reduces competition among birds who frequently forage together. Nuthatches cache nuts and seeds for the winter months.

Nuthatches are named for the way that they use their bills to open seeds or nuts. They'll wedge them in a crevice, like a bark crack, and hammer them open with their bills. They hatch out food the way they "hatched" out of their own eggs.

49. NORTHERN CARDINALS ATTACK THEIR REFLECTION

The Northern Cardinal is the state bird of seven eastern states (but not Michigan. The American Robin is our state bird.) It had always been abundant in the American southeast. Bird feeding with black oil sunflower seeds has slowly increased their range north. It prefers brushy and semi-open habitats, anywhere it can find dense bushes for nesting.

Cardinals are very territorial and aggressive to other cardinals during mating season. One year I had a cardinal see his reflection in one of my windows. He returned each day for two weeks to intimidate and peck at this imaginary interloper.

This is a striking bird, one of the most colorful we have in North America. Males are bright, brilliant red, with a black mask. Females are light brown, looking very beautiful when seen through binoculars, where you can appreciate their subtle red accents. Both sport a pointy feather crest and have long, animated tails. Their stout conical beaks are specially designed to crack open seeds and nutshells.

Northern Cardinals get their red coloration from yellow, orange, and red organic pigments, called carotenoids. An enzyme in the birds' bodies transforms yellow and orange carotenoids to red. Occasionally, a rare genetic mutation occurs and prevents the enzyme from making the color change, and cardinals appear yellow. They still retain that distinctive black mask. Very few yellow Northern Cardinals are seen each year.

Northern Cardinals do not migrate. In early spring, the cardinal courtship begins. Males and females sing together and the male will feed his mate. Together they defend a territory of about 3 acres, chasing off all other males and females.

50. IS THAT A RAVEN OR A CROW?

Members of the crow family (corvids) are so ubiquitous in the suburban landscape that we forget or neglect to watch them, even though they are infinitely more interesting than many other avians. They thrive on human activity. Our garbage and roadkill feed them, and human encroachment has reduced the raptors that devour them. Even agricultural areas are relatively safe; they are smart enough to outsmart farmers. They are opportunistic feeders.

Not only do they thrive in our environment, but they have penetrated our vocabulary with their skills. We tear things apart with "crowbars", we "eat crow", or become "ravenous." The highest point on ships is the "crow's nest."

It can be a challenge to identify a crow vs a raven, especially because we don't see them side-by-side. A raven is twice the size of a crow; it's about the size of a Red-tailed Hawk. Look for differences in their tail feathers. When a crow flies, its tail feathers spread out and look like a fan. When a raven's tail feathers are spread out, it is a more angular wedge shape. If you see the bird perched, look at the throat feathers. Ravens have long throat feathers called hackles, which they can use for a variety of displays. Crows have smooth throat feathers typical of other songbirds.

There are other differences. Ravens and crows fly differently. Crows flap their wings; ravens ride the thermal currents in the atmosphere. Both species are very vocal and have different voices. Crows call out "caw-caw" and make a purring call. A raven will have a deep, hollow croak.

Members of the corvid family are among the smartest birds. Crows and ravens use tools and can be taught (by humans or other birds) to use tools. Crows have a curious memory for human faces and have demonstrated (by experiments) that they recognize and remember humans who are a threat. Crows are more cautious (than ravens) with humans they have never encountered before, but are more comfortable with humans they recognize.

American Crows are widely distributed throughout the state. Ravens are common in the Upper Peninsula of Michigan. There is a lively flock of American Crows living on the University of Michigan campus and surroundings in Ann Arbor. An estimated 10,000 crows return to Ann Arbor each winter, coming from neighboring farms and Canada. On the U of M campus, the buildings are warm and bright lights make it easier to find food. The crows are annoying but not dangerous. The flock will leave around mid-March, as the weather starts to warm up.

OTHER RESOURCES

Websites
allaboutbirds.org
audubon.org
birds.com
birdsanctuary.kbs.msu.edu
birdwatchersdigest.com
detroitriverhawkwatch.org
fws.gov/refuge/shiawassee
gl.audubon.org
identify.whatbird.com
ijc.org
mackinacraptorwatch.org
mlive.com
penguins.detroitzoo.org
sleepingbearbirdingtrail.org
whatbird.com
www.canr.msu.edu
www.trumpeterswansociety.org

Books
Peterson, Roger Tory. *A Field Guide to the Birds a Completely New Guide to All the Birds of Eastern and Central North America.* Houghton Mifflin, 1987.

Sibley, David, et al. *The Sibley Guide to Bird Life and Behavior.* Alfred A. Knopf, 2001.
Kaufman, Kenneth. Lives of North American Birds. Houghton Mifflin, 1997.
Stephenson, Tom, et al. *The Warbler Guide.* Princeton University Press, 2015.
Marzluff, John M., and Tony Angell. *In the Company of Crows and Ravens.* Yale University Press, 2007.

IMAGE SOURCES

1. https://pixabay.com/photos/pied-billed-grebe-bird-animal-swim-6518025/
2. https://pixabay.com/photos/osprey-bird-raptor-3746166/
3. https://pixabay.com/photos/wood-duck-duck-bird-waterfowl-6956019/
4. https://pixabay.com/photos/common-loon-great-northern-diver-5291143/
5. https://pixabay.com/photos/piping-plover-endangered-beach-bird-3615164/
6. https://pixabay.com/photos/white-american-aerial-pelican-386965/
7. https://pixabay.com/photos/hooded-merganser-duck-bird-nature-5061356/
8. https://pixabay.com/photos/heron-waterbird-bird-wading-bird-3454804/
9. By Basar - Own work, CC BY-SA 3.0,
    https://commons.wikimedia.org/w/index.php?curid=9221523
10. By Rhododendrites - Own work, CC BY-SA 4.0,
    https://commons.wikimedia.org/w/index.php?curid=112246946
11. https://pixabay.com/photos/gull-seagull-pacific-gull-4123912/
12. https://pixabay.com/photos/kingfisher-bird-branch-perched-6222453/
13. https://pixabay.com/photos/motion-water-nature-flying-animal-4265082/
14. https://pixabay.com/photos/common-tern-tern-sea-swallow-5138684/
15. https://pixabay.com/photos/bird-sandpiper-beach-shore-sand-944883/
16. https://pixabay.com/photos/birds-bluebird-nature-perch-1232411/
17. https://pixabay.com/photos/common-pheasant-pheasant-3329094/
18. https://pixabay.com/photos/birds-turkey-vulture-wildlife-5080623/
19. https://pixabay.com/photos/wildlife-turkey-wild-turkey-6202054/
20. https://pixabay.com/photos/hedwig-harry-potter-white-snowy-owl-2431460/
21. https://pixabay.com/photos/sandhill-crane-mating-dance-4830984/
22. https://pixabay.com/photos/american-kestrel-nature-wildlife-4053922/
23. https://pixabay.com/photos/bird-towhee-wildlife-birding-wild-5404151/
24. https://pixabay.com/photos/yellow-billed-cuckoo-nature-birds-6922077/
25. https://pixabay.com/photos/bird-ornithology-red-eyed-vireo-7005389/
26. https://pixabay.com/photos/scarlet-tanager-bird-red-bird-5853290/
27. https://pixabay.com/photos/calendula-regulus-bied-kinglet-387070/
28. https://pixabay.com/photos/red-shouldered-hawk-talons-raptor-3754802/
29. https://pixabay.com/photos/prothonotary-warbler-songbird-6988421/
30. https://pixabay.com/photos/pileated-woodpecker-birds-big-birds-3537684/
31. https://pixabay.com/photos/ovenbird-bird-animal-warbler-7000472/
32. https://pixabay.com/photos/flicker-bird-animal-5696212/
33. https://pixabay.com/photos/bird-ruffed-grouse-beak-feathers-7011175/
34. https://pixabay.com/photos/barred-owl-black-eyes-birds-nature-6883524/

35. By Jeol Trick of U.S. Fish and Wildlife Service Headquarters - Endangered Kirtland's warbler (Dendroica kirtlandii)Uploaded by snowmanradio, CC BY 2.0, https://commons.wikimedia.org/w/index.php?curid=18151568
36. https://pixabay.com/photos/indigo-bunting-bird-blue-bird-6307283/
37. https://pixabay.com/photos/nature-bird-woodpecker-bokeh-4573036/
38. https://pixabay.com/photos/wren-carolina-wren-bird-nature-3619826/
39. https://pixabay.com/photos/baltimore-oriole-bird-spring-4218100/
40. https://pixabay.com/photos/tree-creeper-shy-creeper-small-bird-4911787/
41. https://pixabay.com/photos/great-crested-flycatcher-bird-branch-6313767/
42. https://pixabay.com/photos/robin-american-robin-redbreast-bird-3159166/
43. https://pixabay.com/photos/birds-ornithology-dark-eyed-junco-6941069/
44. https://pixabay.com/photos/chickadee-black-capped-chickadee-4419786/
45. https://pixabay.com/photos/spizella-passerina-chipping-sparrow-6316561/
46. https://pixabay.com/photos/hummingbird-bird-hummingbird-feeder-5528673/
47. https://pixabay.com/photos/nuthatch-bird-nature-blue-feathers-5079485/
48. https://pixabay.com/photos/bird-redbird-cardinal-songbird-5357194/

READ OTHER
50 THINGS TO KNOW ABOUT BIRDS IN THE UNITED STATES BOOKS

CZYKPublishing.com

Printed in Great Britain
by Amazon